HOW WILL THEY GET THAT HEART DOWN YOUR THROAT?

 A Child's View of Transplants

by Karen Walton

with illustrations by Allison Patrice Peterson

E.M. Press, Inc.
Manassas, VA

ISBN: 1-880664-99-2
Library of Congress Catalog Card Number: 97-19401

E.M. Press, Inc.
P.O. Box 4057
Manassas, VA 20108

DEDICATION

This book is dedicated to a special person who cared to share—my heart donor, and to her family who honored her wishes.

ACKNOWLEDGEMENTS

To my husband, Jimmy, who could always make me laugh.
To Stacey and Amanda who always gave me reasons to be proud.

To Dr. Leet, Dr. Friehling and Dr. Del Negro who kept me going. To Dr. Burton who did my surgery.

To the faculty, administration and especially the children of Highland School who supported me in so many ways.

To the wonderful and caring staff of Fauquier and Fairfax hospitals in Virginia.

To the Transplant Team at Fairfax Hospital: Dr. Kiernan, Dr. Miller, Paige, Mary Beth, Jasmine and Linda.

And especially to Beth who believed in me and encouraged me to write this book.

Karen

DEDICATION

To our spirited daughter, Lauren Patrice Peterson, who helps me daily to see the world through her eyes.

To Althea and Bill Napolitano, my mom and dad, who have always given me the love and encouragement to be spirited myself.

ACKNOWLEDGEMENTS

Special thanks to Lauren for all her artistic help; to Karen and Charles for their advice and support; to my husband, David, for his quiet encouragement; and especially to Karen and Beth for inviting me to share this journey.

A. P. P.

There was something wrong in the kindergarten class that Mrs. Logan and Mrs. Walton taught together. Mrs. Walton was missing! Where was she? Was she hiding? Was she still asleep in her bed? Everyone was asking Mrs. Logan, "Where is Mrs. Walton?"

Mrs. Logan sat the children down in a circle on the rug. She explained that Mrs. Walton was in the hospital. Everyone started asking questions at once. After Mrs. Logan quieted the children down, she started telling them about Mrs. Walton's sick heart. She told the kindergarteners that Mrs. Walton had been sick for about five years, but now the time had come for her to receive a very special gift.

"A gift? What kind of gift?"

"Mrs. Walton loves jelly beans," said Meghan. "I bet someone is giving her jelly beans."

"No," answered Mrs. Logan, "Mrs. Walton's gift will be an even more special one, a gift of a new heart."

"A new heart? How can someone give anyone a new heart?" the children wanted to know.

Parker asked, "Where does the new heart come from?"

Lauren volunteered her mother to buy Mrs. Walton a new heart at Giant grocery store.

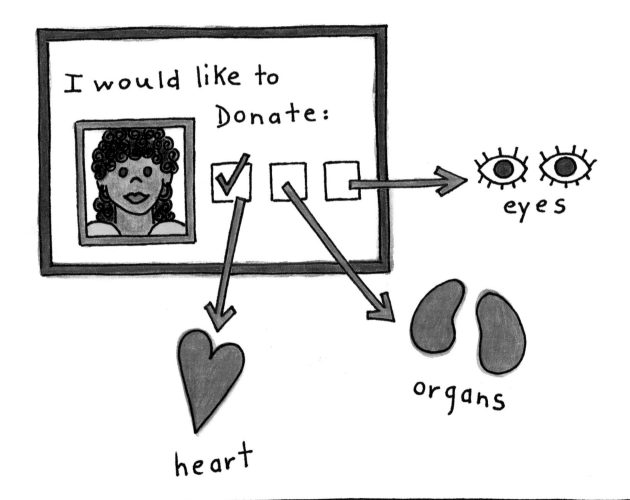

I would like to
Donate:

☑ ☐ ☐ → eyes

heart

organs

Mrs. Logan said that it would not be quite that easy. Very gently she explained that the heart would come from a person who had died, someone who, when alive, had made a decision to share parts of his or her body with someone who needed them like Mrs. Walton did.

"That person," Mrs. Logan explained, "had signed a special piece of paper called a donor card to let the doctors know about his or her decision. Some sick people can get a new and healthy heart, a liver, kidneys, pancreas, skin, or corneas."

Parker said he was very relieved that the person was dead.

Mrs. Logan also explained that anyone who dies can be a donor, even a child. "No one likes to think of anyone dying, especially a child," she said, "but it happens. Then it's the parents who make the decision to share their child's organs."

A kindergartener or two wiggled and squirmed.

"It could bring comfort to them to know their special child saved someone else's child from dying. It is as if a part of their child lives on. Big kids who understand about organ donation can talk to their parents about this important decision. It's good to talk about even the hard things."

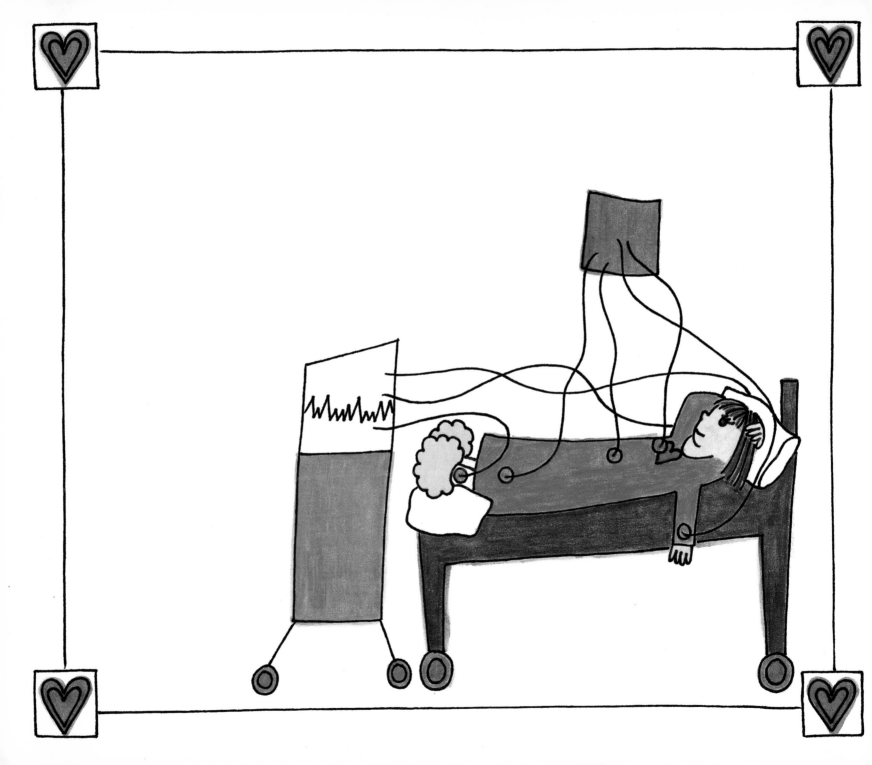

"Mrs. Walton will have to wait in the hospital away from her family and friends. Because her heart is so sick, Mrs. Walton will have to be hooked up to tubes that will keep medicine going into her body. And waiting," Mrs. Logan reminded the class, "is not easy."

Mrs. Walton wanted to go home, but she knew that she needed to stay in the hospital. She received so many wonderful cards from children from her school as well as from other schools. Everyone wished her well—that support is what made the waiting easier.

Some of Mrs. Walton's children from school visited her in her hospital room to cheer her up. Everyone was so very curious about all the buttons and gadgets in her room. One of her kindergarteners, Jackie, came in to visit and, after staring at Mrs. Walton for a long time, asked her, "How will they get that heart down your throat?"

Mrs. Walton laughed and told Jackie that the heart would not be pushed down her throat, but that the doctors would first put her to sleep, then cut open her chest, take out the sick heart and put in the healthy heart.

Jackie thought that her way would be better because the doctors' way would be too yucky. Mrs. Walton agreed.

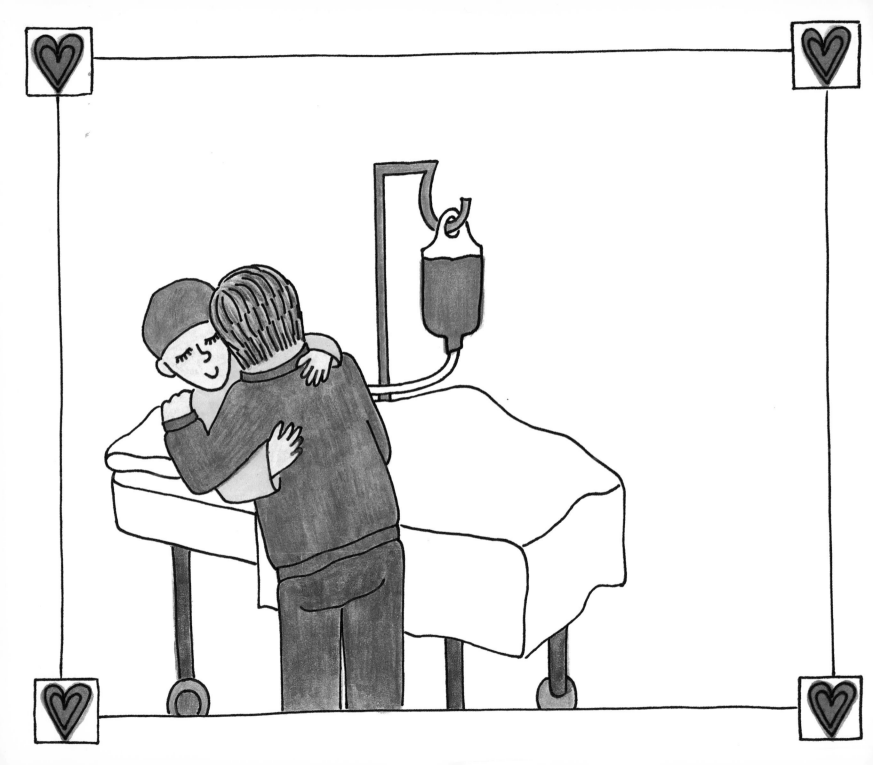

Finally, on May 30, 1995, the long wait was over. A nurse came rushing in to tell Mrs. Walton that a heart was available and ready to be transplanted into her body. The doctors and the nurses were now in a hurry to get their patient ready to go into the operating room. Mr. Walton was able to get to the hospital in time to see Mrs. Walton and give her a hug and a kiss. The last thing that she remembered was a doctor telling her she was going to get sleepy....

The next second, or so it seemed to Mrs. Walton, she opened her eyes to see her husband, sister and her minister standing around her in an intensive care room. It was wonderful to see them and she said a little prayer of thanks to God for letting her open her eyes. It was dark and there were machines in every corner of the room. There were tubes and wires hooked up to Mrs. Walton's body. Something surprising was happening: Mrs. Walton could feel each beat of the new, strong heart.

Oddly, Mrs. Walton felt as if this heart were not really her heart, but that it belonged to someone else. A nurse firmly told her that it was indeed her heart now and she needed to take care of it like the precious gift that it was. After that, Mrs. Walton always called the heart *her* heart.

How To
Take Care
Of Your
New Heart

After the transplant, Mrs. Walton stayed in the hospital for about 17 days. She needed to heal from the surgery, but she also had to learn how to take care of her new heart. Her nurse, Paige, told her that she would have to eat the right foods. Exercise was also important to keep the heart in tip-top shape. Paige had to teach Mrs. Walton about her medicine. Mrs. Walton needed to know how many pills to take and when. She would have to take many of the pills for the rest of her life.

"At least the medicine doesn't taste bad," said Mrs. Walton. "But why do I have to take it?"

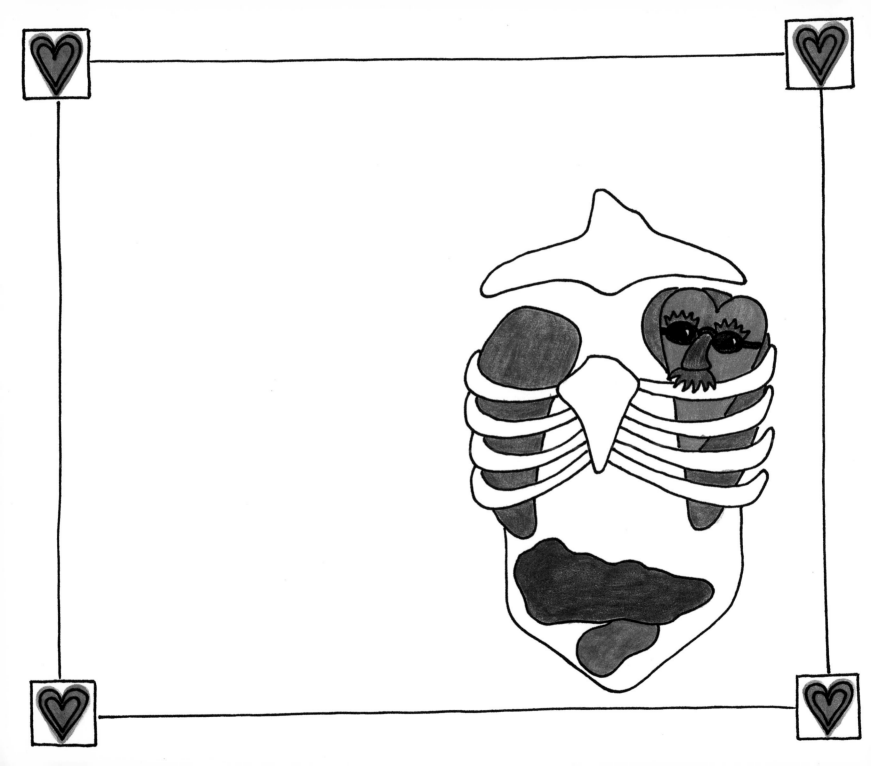

"The body's job is to fight off or reject things that it thinks don't belong inside," explained Paige. "The body will try to get rid of your new heart. The medicine has to trick the body by hiding the heart so the body will leave it alone."

It made Mrs. Walton laugh to think of her body playing "Hide and Seek" with her new heart.

Mrs. Walton had spent three months in the hospital, but now she was going home. She couldn't wait to be with Mr. Walton and her two daughters, Stacey and Amanda. Mr. Walton even had a surprise for her. He and some of his friends had built Mrs. Walton a fish pond, something she had wanted for a long time. When she saw it, Mrs. Walton cried. Mr. Walton thought something was wrong.

"No," said Mrs. Walton. "I am just so happy." It was great to hug Stacey and Amanda and to know that she was going to be there with them for a long, long time.

At first it was a little scary for Mrs. Walton because she needed to be so careful not to be around germs. She'd been told she could get sick very quickly because the medicine she took did not allow her body to fight off the germs and viruses that other people could easily fight off. She had to wear a mask and rubber gloves when she went out or if someone around her was ill. Sometimes the odd way a person looked at her when she had on a mask and gloves hurt her feelings, but she just told herself that they didn't understand.

Each day was better and better. Mrs. Walton's new heart and her body were getting used to each other. Soon Mrs. Walton was able to do some of the things that she liked to do, like fix Amanda's birthday breakfast or walk Josie, their German shepherd, with Stacey. It was even fun to be able to wash dishes once again. She was feeling so well that she wanted to do everything. When the doctor told her that she should wait a year before going back to work as a teacher, Mrs. Walton was sad, but she knew that she had to rest and let her body get well. She thought of all the time she now had to do the many things that she had been thinking of doing while she was in the hospital.

One thing that Mrs. Walton wanted to do was talk to people about donating their organs to help sick people, just like someone had helped her. So she started going to schools, churches and to organizations to tell people about the special gift she had received because someone had cared to share.

"In a time when we recycle everything including plastic, aluminum, trash and glass, why shouldn't we recycle our bodies?" Mrs. Walton asked her audiences. It made her feel good when people told her that they had signed their organ donor cards.

Another thing Mrs. Walton was able to do just months after her surgery was visit her school as a weekly volunteer with the reading program. She loved being with the children and always looked forward to that special day. She was able to visit with her students from the year before who were now big first-graders and get lots of hugs.

On Mrs. Walton's first year transplant anniversary, she received a big surprise, a birthday party for her new heart. Many of the classes sang songs while Mrs. Hicklin played her guitar. Some of the children read poems they had written. Mrs. Walton was given lots of beautiful cards. Best of all, there was a huge cake with one candle on it. When she blew out her candle, the children asked, "What did you wish for?"

"I have already received my wish," said Mrs. Walton. "I'm here with you and my family and friends. What more could I want?"

"How about a piece of cake?" asked one of the children hopefully.

"Great!" said Mrs. Walton. Mrs. Hewitt and Mrs. Burroughs cut a piece of cake for everyone. It was delicious. Mrs. Walton now celebrates two birthdays every year. Isn't she lucky?

Mrs. Walton is back now teaching kindergarten with Mrs. Logan. Her days are busy with her students. And her daughters, Stacey and Amanda, keep her busy too. They go shopping together, go to the movies, or just sit around talking. Mrs. Walton even tried roller blading, tennis and dirt biking!

Mrs. Walton takes very good care of her new heart. And she continues to tell people, young and old, about the special gift of organ donation that makes every new day a special day for her.